50 Authentic Mexican Recipes for Home

By: Kelly Johnson

Table of Contents

- Tacos al Pastor
- Carnitas Tacos
- Chiles Rellenos
- Enchiladas Verdes
- Enchiladas Rojas
- Tamales
- Pozole Rojo
- Pozole Verde
- Birria Tacos
- Sopa de Tortilla
- Cochinita Pibil
- Mole Poblano
- Tinga de Pollo
- Carne Asada
- Barbacoa
- Chiles en Nogada
- Sopes
- Gorditas
- Tostadas de Tinga
- Ceviche de Camarón
- Aguachile
- Pambazos
- Elotes (Mexican Street Corn)
- Esquites (Mexican Corn Salad)
- Caldo de Res
- Caldo Tlalpeño
- Albondigas (Mexican Meatball Soup)
- Camarones a la Diabla
- Queso Fundido
- Chicharrón en Salsa Verde
- Papas con Chorizo
- Huevos Rancheros
- Chilaquiles Verdes
- Chilaquiles Rojos
- Nopales Asados

- Ensalada de Nopales
- Arroz a la Mexicana
- Frijoles Charros
- Menudo
- Flautas de Pollo
- Empanadas de Picadillo
- Huaraches
- Tlayudas
- Camarones al Mojo de Ajo
- Quesadillas de Huitlacoche
- Capirotada (Mexican Bread Pudding)
- Buñuelos
- Tres Leches Cake
- Conchas (Mexican Sweet Bread)
- Champurrado (Mexican Chocolate Atole)

Tacos al Pastor

Ingredients:

- 2 lbs (900g) pork shoulder, thinly sliced
- 3 dried guajillo chiles, deseeded
- 2 dried ancho chiles, deseeded
- 2 chipotle chiles in adobo
- 3 cloves garlic
- ½ cup (120ml) orange juice
- ¼ cup (60ml) pineapple juice
- ¼ cup (60ml) white vinegar
- 1 tablespoon achiote paste
- 1 teaspoon cumin
- 1 teaspoon oregano
- 1 teaspoon salt
- 1 cup pineapple chunks
- Corn tortillas

Instructions:

1. Soak dried chiles in hot water for 10 minutes. Blend with chipotle, garlic, juices, vinegar, achiote, cumin, oregano, and salt.
2. Marinate pork for at least 4 hours or overnight.
3. Grill or pan-fry until charred and cooked through.
4. Serve on corn tortillas with pineapple chunks, onion, and cilantro.

Carnitas Tacos

Ingredients:

- 3 lbs (1.3kg) pork shoulder, cut into chunks
- 1 orange, halved
- 4 cloves garlic
- 1 teaspoon salt
- 1 teaspoon cumin
- 1 teaspoon oregano
- 2 cups (480ml) water
- 2 tablespoons lard

Instructions:

1. Place pork, orange, garlic, salt, cumin, oregano, and water in a pot. Simmer uncovered for 2 hours.
2. Remove pork and shred. Fry in lard until crispy.
3. Serve on corn tortillas with cilantro, onion, and salsa.

Chiles Rellenos

Ingredients:

- 4 poblano peppers
- 8 oz (225g) queso fresco or Monterey Jack cheese
- 3 eggs, separated
- ½ cup (60g) flour
- 1 cup (240ml) tomato sauce
- 1 teaspoon cumin
- 1 teaspoon salt
- ½ cup (120ml) vegetable oil

Instructions:

1. Roast poblanos over open flame, peel skins, and remove seeds.
2. Stuff with cheese and close with toothpicks.
3. Beat egg whites to stiff peaks, fold in yolks.
4. Dust poblanos in flour, dip in egg, and fry in oil until golden.
5. Simmer tomato sauce with cumin and salt, then pour over chiles.

Enchiladas Verdes

Ingredients:

- 12 corn tortillas
- 2 cups (480ml) salsa verde
- 2 cups (200g) shredded chicken
- ½ cup (120ml) sour cream
- 1 cup (120g) crumbled queso fresco
- ½ cup (60g) chopped cilantro

Instructions:

1. Warm tortillas and dip in salsa verde.
2. Fill with chicken, roll up, and place in a baking dish.
3. Pour remaining salsa verde over enchiladas.
4. Top with sour cream, queso fresco, and cilantro.

Enchiladas Rojas

Ingredients:

- 12 corn tortillas
- 2 cups (480ml) red enchilada sauce
- 2 cups (200g) shredded beef or chicken
- 1 cup (120g) shredded cheese
- ½ cup (60g) chopped onion

Instructions:

1. Warm tortillas and dip in enchilada sauce.
2. Fill with meat, roll up, and place in a baking dish.
3. Pour remaining sauce over enchiladas and top with cheese.
4. Bake at 350°F (175°C) for 15 minutes. Garnish with onions.

Tamales

Ingredients:

- 3 cups (375g) masa harina
- 2 teaspoons baking powder
- 1 teaspoon salt
- 1 cup (240ml) lard or butter
- 1 ½ cups (360ml) chicken broth
- 20 dried corn husks

For the filling:

- 2 cups (200g) shredded chicken or pork
- 1 cup (240ml) red or green salsa

Instructions:

1. Soak corn husks in warm water for 30 minutes.
2. Beat lard until fluffy, then mix in masa, baking powder, salt, and broth.
3. Spread masa on corn husks, add filling, and roll up.
4. Steam for 1 hour until firm.

Pozole Rojo

Ingredients:

- 2 lbs (900g) pork shoulder, cubed
- 6 cups (1.4L) chicken broth
- 3 dried guajillo chiles, deseeded
- 2 dried ancho chiles, deseeded
- 3 cloves garlic
- 1 teaspoon oregano
- 1 teaspoon cumin
- 1 can (25 oz) hominy, drained

Instructions:

1. Blend soaked guajillo, ancho, garlic, oregano, and cumin with broth.
2. Simmer pork in broth for 1 ½ hours.
3. Add hominy and blended chile sauce. Simmer 30 more minutes.
4. Serve with radishes, cabbage, lime, and oregano.

Pozole Verde

Ingredients:

- 2 lbs (900g) chicken, cut into pieces
- 6 cups (1.4L) chicken broth
- 1 cup (150g) tomatillos, husked
- 2 poblano peppers
- 2 cloves garlic
- 1 teaspoon cumin
- 1 can (25 oz) hominy, drained

Instructions:

1. Blend tomatillos, poblanos, garlic, cumin, and broth.
2. Simmer chicken in broth for 1 hour.
3. Add hominy and blended sauce. Simmer 30 more minutes.
4. Serve with avocado, lime, and cilantro.

Birria Tacos

Ingredients:

- 3 lbs (1.3kg) beef chuck roast
- 3 dried guajillo chiles, deseeded
- 2 dried ancho chiles, deseeded
- 3 cloves garlic
- 1 teaspoon cumin
- 1 teaspoon oregano
- ½ teaspoon cinnamon
- 2 cups (480ml) beef broth
- Corn tortillas

Instructions:

1. Blend soaked guajillo, ancho, garlic, cumin, oregano, cinnamon, and broth.
2. Marinate beef overnight.
3. Slow-cook for 3 hours until tender. Shred meat.
4. Dip tortillas in broth, fill with beef, and pan-fry until crispy.
5. Serve with broth for dipping.

Sopa de Tortilla

Ingredients:

- 6 corn tortillas, cut into strips
- 4 cups (1L) chicken broth
- 2 tomatoes, chopped
- 1 small onion, chopped
- 2 cloves garlic
- 1 dried guajillo chile, deseeded
- 1 teaspoon cumin
- 1 teaspoon salt
- ½ cup (120ml) oil
- 1 avocado, diced
- ½ cup (120g) queso fresco, crumbled

Instructions:

1. Fry tortilla strips in oil until crispy, then drain on paper towels.
2. Blend tomatoes, onion, garlic, guajillo chile, cumin, and salt.
3. Simmer in broth for 15 minutes.
4. Serve with tortilla strips, avocado, and queso fresco.

Cochinita Pibil

Ingredients:

- 3 lbs (1.3kg) pork shoulder, cut into chunks
- ½ cup (120ml) orange juice
- ¼ cup (60ml) lime juice
- ¼ cup (60ml) white vinegar
- 3 tablespoons achiote paste
- 1 teaspoon cumin
- 1 teaspoon oregano
- 1 teaspoon salt
- Banana leaves (optional)

Instructions:

1. Blend orange juice, lime juice, vinegar, achiote, cumin, oregano, and salt.
2. Marinate pork overnight.
3. Wrap pork in banana leaves and bake at 325°F (160°C) for 3 hours.
4. Shred and serve with pickled onions and tortillas.

Mole Poblano

Ingredients:

- 3 dried guajillo chiles, deseeded
- 3 dried ancho chiles, deseeded
- 2 tablespoons oil
- ½ cup (75g) almonds
- ¼ cup (35g) raisins
- 1 small onion, chopped
- 2 cloves garlic
- 1 small tortilla, toasted
- 1 teaspoon cumin
- 1 teaspoon cinnamon
- 1 ounce (30g) dark chocolate
- 4 cups (1L) chicken broth

Instructions:

1. Toast chiles, almonds, raisins, onion, garlic, tortilla, and spices in oil.
2. Blend with broth until smooth.
3. Simmer for 20 minutes, then stir in chocolate.
4. Serve over chicken or turkey.

Tinga de Pollo

Ingredients:

- 2 cups (200g) shredded chicken
- 1 small onion, sliced
- 2 tomatoes, chopped
- 2 chipotle chiles in adobo
- 2 cloves garlic
- 1 teaspoon oregano
- 1 teaspoon salt
- 2 tablespoons oil

Instructions:

1. Blend tomatoes, chipotles, garlic, oregano, and salt.
2. Sauté onion in oil, then add sauce and simmer for 10 minutes.
3. Stir in shredded chicken and cook for 5 more minutes.
4. Serve on tostadas or with rice.

Carne Asada

Ingredients:

- 2 lbs (900g) skirt steak
- ½ cup (120ml) orange juice
- ¼ cup (60ml) lime juice
- ¼ cup (60ml) olive oil
- 2 cloves garlic, minced
- 1 teaspoon cumin
- 1 teaspoon salt

Instructions:

1. Mix marinade ingredients and marinate steak for 2 hours.
2. Grill over high heat for 3-4 minutes per-side.
3. Slice thinly and serve with tortillas.

Barbacoa

Ingredients:

- 3 lbs (1.3kg) beef cheek or chuck
- 3 dried guajillo chiles, deseeded
- 2 dried ancho chiles, deseeded
- 2 cloves garlic
- 1 teaspoon cumin
- 1 teaspoon oregano
- ½ cup (120ml) white vinegar
- 1 cup (240ml) beef broth

Instructions:

1. Blend soaked guajillo, ancho, garlic, cumin, oregano, vinegar, and broth.
2. Marinate beef overnight.
3. Slow-cook at 275°F (135°C) for 6 hours.
4. Shred and serve with tortillas.

Chiles en Nogada

Ingredients:
For the filling:

- 4 poblano peppers
- 1 lb (450g) ground beef
- ½ cup (75g) chopped almonds
- ½ cup (75g) raisins
- ½ teaspoon cinnamon
- 1 teaspoon salt

For the sauce:

- 1 cup (240ml) heavy cream
- ½ cup (75g) walnuts
- ¼ cup (60ml) milk
- 1 teaspoon sugar

Instructions:

1. Roast and peel poblano peppers.
2. Cook beef with almonds, raisins, cinnamon, and salt.
3. Stuff peppers with beef mixture.
4. Blend sauce ingredients and pour over peppers. Garnish with pomegranate seeds.

Sopes

Ingredients:

- 2 cups (250g) masa harina
- 1 cup (240ml) warm water
- ½ teaspoon salt

Instructions:

1. Mix masa harina, water, and salt into a dough.
2. Shape into small discs and cook on a hot skillet for 2 minutes per side.
3. Pinch edges to form a rim and fry in oil until crispy.
4. Top with beans, meat, cheese, and salsa.

Gorditas

Ingredients:

- 2 cups (250g) masa harina
- 1 cup (240ml) warm water
- ½ teaspoon salt
- ½ cup (120ml) oil

Instructions:

1. Mix masa harina, water, and salt into a dough.
2. Shape into thick discs and cook on a skillet for 3 minutes per side.
3. Cut open and fill with beans, cheese, or meat.

Tostadas de Tinga

Ingredients:

- 6 corn tortillas
- 2 cups (200g) shredded chicken tinga (see recipe above)
- ½ cup (120g) sour cream
- ½ cup (120g) queso fresco, crumbled

Instructions:

1. Fry tortillas in oil until crispy.
2. Top with tinga, sour cream, and queso fresco.

Ceviche de Camarón

Ingredients:

- 1 lb (450g) shrimp, diced
- ½ cup (120ml) lime juice
- 1 small red onion, finely chopped
- 1 tomato, diced
- 1 jalapeño, chopped
- ¼ cup (60g) cilantro, chopped
- ½ teaspoon salt

Instructions:

1. Marinate shrimp in lime juice for 30 minutes.
2. Mix with onion, tomato, jalapeño, cilantro, and salt.
3. Serve with tostadas or crackers.

Aguachile

Ingredients:

- 1 lb (450g) raw shrimp, peeled and deveined
- ½ cup (120ml) lime juice
- 2 serrano chiles, chopped
- ¼ cup (60ml) water
- ½ teaspoon salt
- ½ cucumber, sliced
- ¼ red onion, thinly sliced
- ¼ cup (15g) cilantro, chopped

Instructions:

1. Blend lime juice, serrano chiles, water, and salt.
2. Marinate shrimp in the mixture for 15 minutes until opaque.
3. Serve with cucumber, red onion, and cilantro.

Pambazos

Ingredients:

- 4 bolillo or telera rolls
- 2 cups (200g) chorizo, cooked
- 2 cups (400g) potatoes, boiled and diced
- 3 guajillo chiles, deseeded
- 1 cup (240ml) water
- 1 clove garlic
- ½ teaspoon salt
- ½ cup (120ml) oil
- Shredded lettuce, crema, and queso fresco for topping

Instructions:

1. Blend guajillo chiles, garlic, water, and salt into a sauce.
2. Mix cooked chorizo with potatoes.
3. Dip bread into guajillo sauce, then pan-fry in oil.
4. Fill with chorizo-potato mixture and top with lettuce, crema, and queso fresco.

Elotes (Mexican Street Corn)

Ingredients:

- 4 ears of corn
- ½ cup (120g) mayonnaise
- ½ cup (120g) crumbled cotija cheese
- 1 teaspoon chili powder
- 1 lime, cut into wedges

Instructions:

1. Grill or boil corn until cooked.
2. Spread with mayonnaise and roll in cotija cheese.
3. Sprinkle with chili powder and serve with lime wedges.

Esquites (Mexican Corn Salad)

Ingredients:

- 2 cups (300g) corn kernels
- 1 tablespoon butter
- ½ cup (120g) mayonnaise
- ½ cup (120g) crumbled cotija cheese
- 1 teaspoon chili powder
- 1 lime, juiced

Instructions:

1. Sauté corn in butter for 5 minutes.
2. Mix with mayonnaise, cotija cheese, chili powder, and lime juice.

Caldo de Res

Ingredients:

- 2 lbs (900g) beef shank or short ribs
- 8 cups (2L) water
- 2 carrots, chopped
- 2 potatoes, chopped
- ½ cabbage, chopped
- 1 zucchini, chopped
- 1 ear of corn, cut into chunks
- 1 small onion, chopped
- 2 cloves garlic
- 1 teaspoon salt
- ½ teaspoon oregano

Instructions:

1. Simmer beef, water, onion, garlic, and salt for 1 ½ hours.
2. Add carrots, potatoes, and corn. Cook for 15 minutes.
3. Add cabbage, zucchini, and oregano. Cook for 10 minutes.

Caldo Tlalpeño

Ingredients:

- 2 cups (200g) shredded chicken
- 6 cups (1.5L) chicken broth
- 2 tomatoes, chopped
- 1 chipotle chile in adobo, chopped
- 1 small onion, chopped
- 2 cloves garlic
- 1 cup (150g) cooked garbanzo beans
- 1 zucchini, chopped
- ½ teaspoon cumin

Instructions:

1. Sauté onion, garlic, and tomatoes. Blend into a sauce.
2. Simmer broth with sauce, chicken, garbanzo beans, zucchini, and cumin for 15 minutes.

Albóndigas (Mexican Meatball Soup)

Ingredients:

For the meatballs:

- 1 lb (450g) ground beef
- ½ cup (50g) rice, uncooked
- 1 egg
- 1 teaspoon salt
- ½ teaspoon cumin

For the broth:

- 6 cups (1.5L) beef broth
- 2 tomatoes, chopped
- 1 carrot, chopped
- 1 potato, chopped
- ½ teaspoon oregano

Instructions:

1. Mix meatball ingredients and shape into balls.
2. Simmer broth with tomatoes, carrot, potato, and oregano.
3. Add meatballs and cook for 30 minutes.

Camarones a la Diabla

Ingredients:

- 1 lb (450g) shrimp, peeled and deveined
- 3 guajillo chiles, deseeded
- 2 chipotle chiles in adobo
- 1 small onion, chopped
- 2 cloves garlic
- ½ teaspoon salt
- 2 tablespoons oil

Instructions:

1. Blend guajillo, chipotle, onion, garlic, and salt into a sauce.
2. Sauté shrimp in oil, then pour sauce over and cook for 5 minutes.

Queso Fundido

Ingredients:

- 2 cups (200g) shredded Oaxaca or Monterey Jack cheese
- ½ cup (100g) cooked chorizo
- 1 small onion, chopped
- 1 small poblano pepper, roasted and chopped

Instructions:

1. Preheat oven to 375°F (190°C).
2. Layer cheese, chorizo, onion, and poblano in a baking dish.
3. Bake for 10 minutes until melted. Serve with tortillas.

Chicharrón en Salsa Verde

Ingredients:

- 2 cups (200g) chicharrón (fried pork rinds)
- 2 cups (480ml) salsa verde
- ½ cup (120ml) chicken broth
- 1 teaspoon salt

Instructions:

1. Heat salsa verde and broth in a pan.
2. Add chicharrón and simmer for 5 minutes.

Papas con Chorizo

Ingredients:

- 2 cups (400g) potatoes, diced
- 1 cup (200g) chorizo
- ½ teaspoon salt
- 2 tablespoons oil

Instructions:

1. Boil potatoes until tender.
2. Sauté chorizo in oil, then add potatoes and salt. Cook for 5 minutes.

Huevos Rancheros

Ingredients:

- 4 corn tortillas
- 4 eggs
- 2 tomatoes, chopped
- 1 small onion, chopped
- 1 serrano chile, chopped
- 1 clove garlic, minced
- ½ teaspoon salt
- ½ cup (120ml) oil

Instructions:

1. Sauté onion, garlic, and serrano chile. Add tomatoes and salt, simmer for 10 minutes.
2. Fry tortillas in oil until slightly crispy.
3. Fry eggs to desired doneness.
4. Place eggs on tortillas and top with salsa.

Chilaquiles Verdes

Ingredients:

- 12 corn tortillas, cut into triangles
- 2 cups (480ml) salsa verde
- ½ cup (120ml) chicken broth
- ½ cup (120g) crema
- ½ cup (100g) crumbled queso fresco
- 2 tablespoons oil

Instructions:

1. Fry tortilla pieces in oil until crispy, then drain.
2. Heat salsa verde and broth, then add tortillas. Stir for 2 minutes.
3. Top with crema and queso fresco.

Chilaquiles Rojos

Ingredients:

- 12 corn tortillas, cut into triangles
- 2 cups (480ml) red enchilada sauce
- ½ cup (120ml) chicken broth
- ½ cup (120g) crema
- ½ cup (100g) crumbled queso fresco
- 2 tablespoons oil

Instructions:

1. Fry tortilla pieces in oil until crispy, then drain.
2. Heat enchilada sauce and broth, then add tortillas. Stir for 2 minutes.
3. Top with crema and queso fresco.

Nopales Asados

Ingredients:

- 4 nopales (cactus paddles), cleaned
- 1 tablespoon olive oil
- ½ teaspoon salt
- ½ teaspoon black pepper

Instructions:

1. Brush nopales with olive oil and season with salt and pepper.
2. Grill for 5 minutes per side until tender.

Ensalada de Nopales

Ingredients:

- 2 nopales, diced
- 1 small tomato, diced
- ¼ cup (30g) chopped onion
- ¼ cup (15g) chopped cilantro
- ½ teaspoon salt
- 1 tablespoon lime juice

Instructions:

1. Boil diced nopales for 10 minutes, then rinse.
2. Mix with tomato, onion, cilantro, salt, and lime juice.

Arroz a la Mexicana

Ingredients:

- 1 cup (200g) long-grain rice
- 2 cups (480ml) chicken broth
- 2 tomatoes, blended
- 1 small onion, chopped
- 1 clove garlic, minced
- 1 teaspoon salt
- 2 tablespoons oil

Instructions:

1. Sauté rice in oil until golden.
2. Add onion, garlic, and blended tomatoes. Cook for 3 minutes.
3. Add broth and salt, cover, and simmer for 20 minutes.

Frijoles Charros

Ingredients:

- 2 cups (400g) pinto beans, cooked
- 4 slices bacon, chopped
- 1 small onion, chopped
- 2 tomatoes, diced
- 1 jalapeño, chopped
- 1 teaspoon cumin
- ½ teaspoon salt

Instructions:

1. Fry bacon, then add onion and jalapeño. Cook for 5 minutes.
2. Add tomatoes, cumin, and salt, then stir in beans.
3. Simmer for 10 minutes.

Menudo

Ingredients:

- 2 lbs (900g) beef tripe, cut into pieces
- 8 cups (2L) water
- 2 dried guajillo chiles, deseeded
- 2 dried ancho chiles, deseeded
- 3 cloves garlic
- 1 teaspoon oregano
- 1 teaspoon salt
- 1 can (25 oz) hominy, drained

Instructions:

1. Boil tripe in water for 2 hours.
2. Blend soaked guajillo, ancho, garlic, oregano, and salt into a sauce.
3. Add sauce and hominy to pot, simmer for 30 minutes.

Flautas de Pollo

Ingredients:

- 12 corn tortillas
- 2 cups (200g) shredded chicken
- ½ cup (120ml) oil
- ½ cup (120g) crema
- ½ cup (100g) crumbled queso fresco

Instructions:

1. Roll chicken inside tortillas and secure with toothpicks.
2. Fry in oil until golden and crispy.
3. Serve with crema and queso fresco.

Empanadas de Picadillo

Ingredients:

For the filling:

- 1 lb (450g) ground beef
- 1 small onion, chopped
- 1 small potato, diced
- 1 teaspoon cumin
- ½ teaspoon salt

For the dough:

- 2 cups (250g) all-purpose flour
- ½ teaspoon salt
- ½ cup (113g) butter, cold and cubed
- ½ cup (120ml) water

Instructions:

1. Sauté onion, beef, potato, cumin, and salt. Let cool.
2. Mix flour, salt, butter, and water into a dough. Roll out and cut circles.
3. Fill with beef mixture, fold, and seal.
4. Bake at 375°F (190°C) for 20 minutes or fry until golden.

Huaraches

Ingredients:

- 2 cups (250g) masa harina
- 1 cup (240ml) warm water
- ½ teaspoon salt

Instructions:

1. Mix masa harina, water, and salt into a dough.
2. Shape into oval huaraches and cook on a hot skillet for 3 minutes per side.
3. Top with beans, meat, lettuce, and salsa.

Tlayudas (Oaxacan-Style Mexican Pizza)

Ingredients:

- 4 large tlayuda tortillas (or extra-large corn tortillas)
- 1 cup (240g) refried black beans
- 1 cup (120g) crumbled queso fresco or Oaxaca cheese
- 1 cup (150g) shredded cabbage or lettuce
- 1 avocado, sliced
- ½ cup (120g) Mexican crema
- ½ lb (225g) chorizo or carne asada
- 1 teaspoon salt

Instructions:

1. Toast the tortillas over medium heat until crispy.
2. Spread refried beans over each tortilla.
3. Top with cheese, shredded cabbage, avocado, crema, and meat.
4. Serve folded or open-faced.

Camarones al Mojo de Ajo (Garlic Shrimp)

Ingredients:

- 1 lb (450g) shrimp, peeled and deveined
- 6 cloves garlic, minced
- ¼ cup (60ml) olive oil or butter
- 2 tablespoons lime juice
- ½ teaspoon salt
- ½ teaspoon black pepper
- ¼ cup (15g) chopped cilantro

Instructions:

1. Heat olive oil or butter in a pan over medium heat.
2. Sauté garlic until fragrant, about 1 minute.
3. Add shrimp, salt, and pepper, cooking until pink (about 3 minutes).
4. Stir in lime juice and cilantro, then serve.

Quesadillas de Huitlacoche (Corn Mushroom Quesadillas)

Ingredients:

- 2 cups (200g) huitlacoche (corn mushroom)
- ½ cup (50g) chopped onion
- 1 serrano chile, chopped
- 1 tablespoon butter
- ½ teaspoon salt
- 8 corn tortillas
- 1 cup (120g) Oaxaca or Monterey Jack cheese

Instructions:

1. Melt butter in a pan and sauté onion, serrano chile, and huitlacoche for 5 minutes.
2. Heat tortillas, fill with huitlacoche mixture and cheese.
3. Fold and cook on a griddle until cheese melts.

Capirotada (Mexican Bread Pudding)

Ingredients:

- 4 cups (400g) bolillo or French bread, cubed
- 1 ½ cups (360ml) piloncillo (or brown sugar) syrup
- 1 teaspoon cinnamon
- ½ teaspoon cloves
- ½ cup (75g) raisins
- ½ cup (50g) chopped pecans
- ½ cup (120g) shredded cheese (queso fresco or Monterey Jack)

Instructions:

1. Preheat oven to 350°F (175°C).
2. Layer bread, raisins, pecans, and cheese in a baking dish.
3. Pour warm piloncillo syrup over the layers.
4. Bake for 25 minutes until golden.

Buñuelos (Mexican Crispy Fritters)

Ingredients:

- 2 cups (250g) all-purpose flour
- ½ teaspoon baking powder
- ½ teaspoon salt
- 2 tablespoons sugar
- 1 tablespoon butter, melted
- ½ cup (120ml) warm water
- ½ teaspoon cinnamon
- ½ cup (100g) sugar for dusting
- Oil for frying

Instructions:

1. Mix flour, baking powder, salt, and sugar. Add butter and warm water to form a dough.
2. Let rest for 30 minutes, then divide into balls.
3. Roll out thin and fry in hot oil until golden.
4. Dust with cinnamon sugar.

Tres Leches Cake

Ingredients:

For the cake:

- 1 cup (125g) all-purpose flour
- 1 teaspoon baking powder
- ¼ teaspoon salt
- 5 eggs, separated
- 1 cup (200g) sugar
- 1 teaspoon vanilla extract
- ⅓ cup (80ml) whole milk

For the milk mixture:

- 1 can (12 oz) evaporated milk
- 1 can (14 oz) sweetened condensed milk
- ½ cup (120ml) heavy cream

For the topping:

- 1 cup (240ml) heavy whipping cream
- 2 tablespoons sugar

Instructions:

1. Preheat oven to 350°F (175°C). Grease a 9x13-inch pan.
2. Beat egg yolks and sugar, then add vanilla and milk. Fold in flour, baking powder, and salt.
3. Beat egg whites until stiff peaks form and fold into batter.
4. Bake for 30 minutes, then poke holes in the cake and pour milk mixture over it.
5. Chill for 4+ hours, then top with whipped cream.

Conchas (Mexican Sweet Bread)

Ingredients:

For the dough:

- 4 cups (500g) bread flour
- ½ cup (100g) sugar
- 1 teaspoon salt
- 2 teaspoons yeast
- ½ cup (120ml) warm milk
- 3 eggs
- ½ cup (113g) butter, softened

For the topping:

- ½ cup (113g) butter, softened
- 1 cup (120g) powdered sugar
- 1 cup (125g) flour
- 1 teaspoon vanilla or cocoa powder

Instructions:

1. Mix flour, yeast, sugar, salt, milk, eggs, and butter. Knead for 10 minutes.
2. Let rise for 2 hours. Divide into balls.
3. Mix topping ingredients, roll into discs, and place on top of dough.
4. Bake at 350°F (175°C) for 20-25 minutes.

Champurrado (Mexican Chocolate Atole)

Ingredients:

- 4 cups (1L) milk
- 2 cups (480ml) water
- ½ cup (75g) masa harina
- ½ cup (100g) piloncillo or brown sugar
- 1 cinnamon stick
- 4 oz (113g) Mexican chocolate, chopped

Instructions:

1. Heat water and dissolve masa harina.
2. Add milk, piloncillo, cinnamon, and chocolate.
3. Simmer and whisk until thickened.